Emerald Lake

CHAPTER 1 INTRODUCTION

The Canadian Rockies are made up of 4 national parks: Banff, Jasper, Yoho, and Kootenay. Banff National Park is huge at 2564 square miles (6641 square Kilometers). Jasper is bigger at 4,200 sq mi (10,900 sq km). The word superlative does not begin to describe the scenery here. This mountain range will blow your mind. From quite strolls along paved paths at Lake Louise to multi-day backpack trips to alpine mountaineering these parks offer something for everyone. This area can be enjoyed on a budget or indulgently and again is open to all.

Bow Summit

Along Icefields Parkwah

ow Lake

Flag Over Banff

Crowfoot Glacier

Mount Edith Cavell

Yellow Ladyslipper

Lake Minnewanka

CHAPTER 2 BANFF

Banff is both the name of the southernmost of the four national parks and of the main town within that national park. The term townsite or Banff townsite will be used when referring to the town to avoid confusion. The townsite is located approximately 75 mi (128 Km) from Calgary. Most flights into the area arrive at Calgary International Airport (YYC). From the airport, it's a very easy drive around Calgary and across the prairie to Banff, it takes about 90 minutes. If following GPS directions the northern route is the shortest and also has the fewest options for food and gasoline. If hungry after a long flight or need to gas up prior to dropping off the rental car consider going through downtown Calgary.

At the edge of the Rocky Mountains sits

Canmore, the first town reached after leaving Calgary. Canmore is a great place to eat, shop and stock up on groceries as prices are a little lower than in the town of Banff. Also the scenery here is amazing, with the Three Sisters range as a backdrop to the town. Many hiking and skiing opportunities can be found in Canmore.

About a 20-minute drive further west brings one to the town of Banff. Banff was first settled in the 1880s when TransCanada railway workers discovered a hot springs in the area. The structures surrounding the hot springs have evolved over the years, but the springs remain a main attraction. Originally, a bathhouse was located near the Cave and Basin, now the upper hot springs house the bathing facility about a mile away (follow the signs to the Sulphur Mountain Gondola and the hot spring pool is adjacent). The Cave and Basin area has interesting historical exhibits. The cave has a small waterfall of hot springs water and is worth a visit on a rainy day, but these springs are for looking at only as they are home to an endangered snail found no where else.

The town has grown significantly since its humble beginnings. Now a major tourist destination in both summer and winter, it still retains a charm often lost with development. The scenery in the town itself is appealing as huge mountains are visible from every angle. The Banff Springs Hotel is a beautiful structure sitting adjacent to the Bow River and above Bow River Falls. The Banff Springs sets a high standard for luxury, but it doesn't come cheap. Slightly above the town, the Sulphur Mountain Gondola whisks visitors up 2800 feet in about 8 minutes to panoramic views of the town, as well as the surrounding mountains. A boardwalk makes for easy walking to several excellent observation areas.

The Gondola is located next to the Upper Hot Springs and a lovely hotel, the Rimrock. We like to stay at the Rimrock for the excellent views, comfortable rooms and nearness to the hot springs and gondola.

The town of Banff offers many eating and shopping opportunities. It also has the many obligatory souvenir shops to pick up a little Canadian Rockies swag. There seem to be an abundance of rock and Gem shops; be sure to check out local ammonite jewelry, mad from fossilized shell creatures. Several art galleries offer paintings by local artists and truly impressive photos of the region. Hotels range from the super fancy (and pricey)

Two Jake Lake

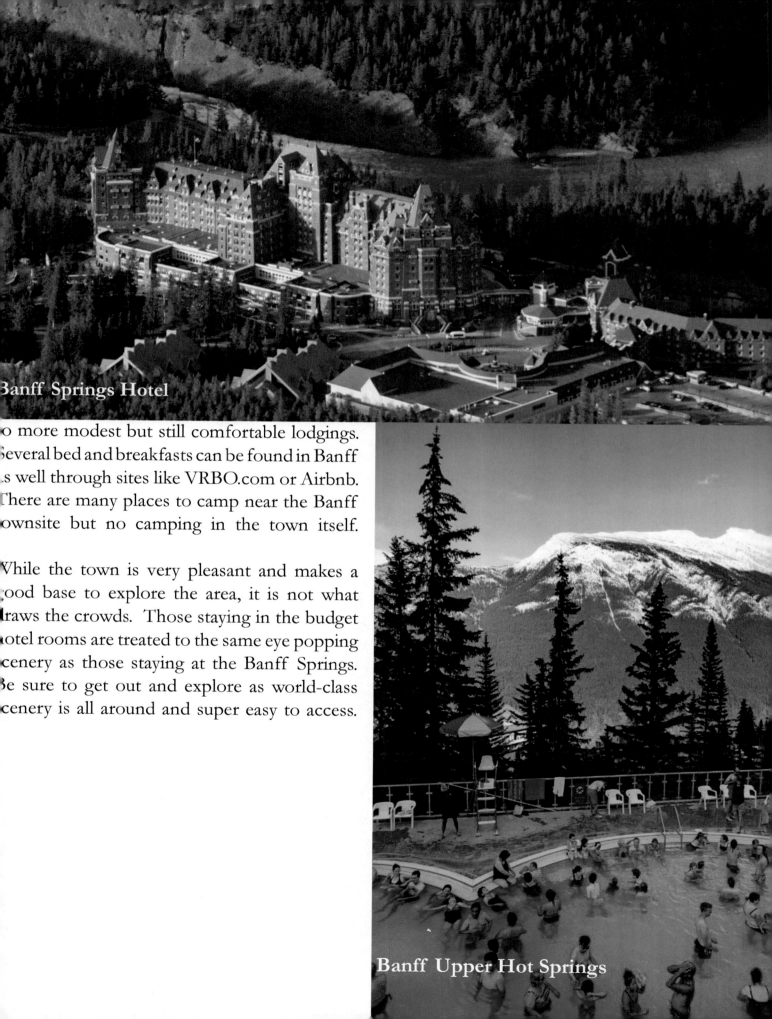

Banff Springs Hotel

o more modest but still comfortable lodgings.
Several bed and breakfasts can be found in Banff
as well through sites like VRBO.com or Airbnb.
There are many places to camp near the Banff
townsite but no camping in the town itself.

While the town is very pleasant and makes a
good base to explore the area, it is not what
draws the crowds. Those staying in the budget
hotel rooms are treated to the same eye popping
scenery as those staying at the Banff Springs.
Be sure to get out and explore as world-class
scenery is all around and super easy to access.

Banff Upper Hot Springs

Cave and Basin National Historic Site

Banff From Gondola Overlook

unset over Banff

Vermillion Lakes

Sunrise over Mt Rundle

From the main highway there are 2 main exits to the town of Banff, the more eastern exit is Banff Avenue. Heading away from the town leads to the Lake Minnewanka Scenic Drive. This motor loop is about 15 miles long and should not be missed. The loop takes visitors past mountain meadows with iconic views of the surrounding mountains. It travels past three lovely lakes: Lake Minnewanka, Two Jack Lake and Johnson Lake. As a glacier fed lake, Minnewanka is a deep ethereal blue, often it is the first such lake encountered in Banff and hints at the wonders in store at Lake Louise and Moraine lake. The scenery shifts and changes with weather and time of day, with the best light often near twilight in morning and evening.

Wildlife encounters are frequent along this stretch of road, especially late in the day. Mountain goats, elk and bears are routinely seen. Swimming is permitted in the lakes but is for stout souls unafraid of glacially cold water.

Back on the highway, the more western exit is Mt Norquay Road. Just after exiting look for a small road heading west. This leads to the Vermillion Lakes. This short drive passes 3 lakes with amazing views of Mt Rundle. If exiting the highway you turn away from town, the road climbs steeply to the Green Spot with excellent views of the mountains and the town of Banff. Travelling to the end of the road arrive at Mt Norquay ski area. From the town of Banff, this is the closest place to ski. During the summer, a delightful chairlift whisks visitors to a great overlook and small restaurant.

Banff from "the Green Spot"

Lake Minnewank Loop Meadow

Two Jack Lake

Johnson Lake

Bow Valley Parkway

CHAPTER 3 BOW VALLEY

Traveling from Banff to the Lake Louise area requires a hard choice, slow and scenic or fast and scenic. If only all choices were this hard. The slower route is via Bow River Parkway. Passing Johnston Canyon, the Parkway meanders past numerous wildflower filled meadows, rewarding mountain views and has many wildlife viewing opportunities. The parkway parallels Route 1 and is two lane driving with multiple pullouts for gawking at the scenery.

Johnston Canyon is about a 30-minute drive from Banff. A lovely glacier fed creek and winds through deep limestone walls cut this canyon. The trail is wide and gently sloped, at places relying on boardwalk bridges built into the sheer rock walls above the flowing water. It is about half mile walk to the lower falls and a mile to

the upper falls. The canyon is worth seeing in any weather, making it a good rainy day choice.

On a recent trip we encountered a bull elk, a large black bear wandering through a meadow and black wolf pups all in one morning. Moose also frequent the area. If pressed for time, Route 1 allows four lane driving at highway speeds. Lake Louise can be reached in about 45 minutes, if you don't stop, but likely you will want to stop.

A diversionary opportunity for sightseeing off Route 1 is the Sunshine Village ski area. In summer, bus trips are available to the Sunshine Meadows, which is a wild flower paradise. Due to the high vv the wildflowers don't really get going until July. The Meadows are lovely, but to

Rainbow over Bow Valley Parkway

reach them you need to plan ahead. The shuttle bus from the ski village to the meadows fills up fast; reservations aren't required but highly recommended. Once to the Meadows, the hiking is easy with rewarding views of Rock Island and down into Mt Assiniboine Provincial Park. The access road to the Sunshine Village has proven an excellent place to encounter bighorn sheep. These sheep are often found near dusk, licking the salt from the roadside. Usually, they are distracted and can be approached fairly closely, but as always be cautious near wildlife.

Turn right at the northern end of the Bow Valley Parkway to head to the Lake Louise Ski area. During the summer months, the ski lifts whisk passengers to an incredibly scenic overlook. The best time for photography is usually before noon. Grizzly bears are known to frequent the meadows beneath the ski lift.

Johnston Canyon

Along Bow Valley Parkway

Canadian Pacific and Bow River

Lake Louise From Ski Overlook

Lake Louise

CHAPTER 4 LAKE LOUISE

Lake Louise is unforgettable. This area, along with Moraine Lake, is the beating heart of the Canadian Rockies; it is why you come to this place. It has it all. Stunning glacier capped mountains loom over perfect, unbelievably blue lakes, and hiking trails that, improbably, are able to improve on the initial views. The stunning vistas are imminently accessible. Just a few feet from the parking areas are some of the most iconic scenes in Canada. Paved trails lead up to and around Lake Louise.

Chateau Lake Louise, a five star luxury hotel, sits immediately adjacent to the lake, the architecture blending well with the sumptuous alpine scenery. In the summer, poppies are planted around the grounds of the hotel adding splashes of dazzling color to a scene already bursting. It seems almost too much to believe. The light changes subtly throughout the day. Early morning light is best for both Lake Louise and Moraine Lake. However, later in the afternoon and on overcast days the rich colors seem deeper. At Lake Louise consider renting a canoe for a quick paddle across the otherworldly blue water. Besides canoeing, there are many opportunities for hiking, with several trails starting at the lakeshore. One of the most popular is the short hike to Lake Agnes Tea House. The trail begins just past the hotel. The trail is wide and smooth, climbing about 1300 ft (400 m) in about 2.2 miles (3.5 km) one way. The teahouse is, well, a teahouse, but set high up in the mountains and appropriately rustic. The trail and teahouse can be quite crowded so be prepared. The tea and snacks are priced as if the person serving them carried them about 2.2 miles, because they did, but tasty nonetheless. The trail continues on to Little Beehive, Big Beehive and the High Line trail.

Another trail originating at Lake Louise is the Plain of Six Glaciers. A longer trek than to Lake Agnes, hikers are similarly rewarded with a remote teahouse. The trip is 3.4 miles (5.5 km) one-way with 1200 ft (370 m) elevation gain. The path for the Plain of Six Glaciers diverges from the Lake Agnes trail and hugs the shoreline. As the trail ascends, the multiple glaciers clinging to Mt Victoria come into better view. A lovely creek cascades past the teahouse with wildflower meadows behind. Both of these hikes can get crowded. Some guidebooks warn against hiking here because of the crowds. These are some of the most popular hikes in Banff and for good reason, who doesn't want overpriced tea in a mind-blowing environment. Even if shared with many others the trails have never felt unpleasantly crowded, but this is not the place to go if looking for solitude.

Paradise Bungalows is a moderately priced hotel a very short distance from Lake Louise. Their gardening skills are evident throughout the summer with poppies, violets, and delphiniums in striking displays. Though a little bit older and fairly close to the road, the rooms were comfortable and equipped with a kitchen. Most of the rooms had two bedrooms, excellent for families. The location was ideal and the street noise died down significantly as the sun went down.

The cascading creek next to the road in this area is another favorite scene. The blue glacial waters tumble down with wildflowers gracing the steep road embankment. With careful framing, the road disappears.

Lake Louise Campground is situated next to the Bow River near the Lake Louise Village. It is large and fills quickly. Lake Louise Village is a good place to fill up on gas, grab some lunch and get groceries If you are in need of more souvenirs, they have you covered as well.

Lake Louise

Roadside Cascade Lake Louise

Lake Louise Area

Lake LouiseBoathouse

Lake Agnes Teahouse

Lake Louise with Poppies

Moraine Lake

CHAPTER 4 MORAINE LAKE

Moraine Lake is my favorite place on earth. It's hard to imagine a more perfect scene, the blue of the lake satisfies my soul, and the Ten Peaks surrounding it are breathtaking. Unbelievably, some seem so focused on Lake Louise that they skip Moraine Lake. To get there, turn off the road-connecting Lake Louise Village to Lake Louise and drive approximately 13 miles (29km).

The glacial lakes in the area are a stunning blue. This is no trick of the camera (something I couldn't quite believe until I saw it myself) but caused by fine particles of rock, called rock flour, suspended in the water. The glaciers pulverize underlying rock as they migrate down the mountains and create this fine powder. The unique limestone of these regions is responsible for the stunning colors. As the

summer passes, the build up of more rock flour changes the color of the lakes, making them very slightly greener. The silt suspended in the water also makes them fairly opaque. The silt combined with cold temperatures and low nutrients make uninviting environments for fish. So while fish are usually present, they are usually small and sparse in number.

The best views of Moraine Lake can be found from atop the rock pile at the near end of the lake. The rock pile allows a quick elevation gain of about one hundred feet and the prettiest scene I have ever seen. Bring the wide-angle lens! This rock pile was originally thought to be a terminal moraine, the pushed up pile of rock and debris marking a glaciers furthest extent, but is now thought to be the remnants

Moraine Lake

of an ancient landslide, which created the lake. So, there are no moraines at Moraine Lake.

The best time of day for photographing the whole amazing scene is earlier in the day. By noon the sun is overhead and then sets behind the mountains lighting the scene from the back. Very late in the day, twilight can be amazing. There is no alpenglow as the sun is still behind the mountains but the soft evening light works well. Also, the lake is often nearly deserted as the tour buses have gone to find dinner elsewhere.

Aside from gawking in wonderment at this slice of heaven, there is quite a bit to do around Moraine Lake. Canoes rentals are available and recommended, even more so than at Lake Louise. The looming peaks loom even more up close. The water under the canoe is incandescent blue.

Many excellent hiking trails originate at Moraine Lake. One of the most famous is the hike to Sentinel Pass. It starts at the parking lot at Moraine Lake, ascends 2400 ft (732m) and is 7.5 miles (12 km) round trip. It is moderately strenuous, especially the last mile or so. The views are memorable, the ten peaks a constant backdrop. From Sentinel Pass, views and trails continue down into Paradise Valley. After a fairly steep initial ascent, the trail levels out and passes Minnestimma Lakes, lovely little reflecting pools. After a respite at these pools, the steeper ascent resumes. In the fall, larch trees along this trail turn golden yellow. Larch trees are deciduous conifers, shedding their needle-leaves each fall. The peak of the color is usually mid to late September. The trail to Sentinel Pass is sometimes called Larch Valley, referring to these trees.

Grizzlies frequent this area. Often, warnings are

posted requiring hikers to travel in groups of 4-6 to discourage unwanted interactions with the bears, be sure to join a group traveling at a similar pace. Typically, trails are not closed for bears here but it would be wise to heed any posted warnings.

Moraine Lake

Moraine Lake

Spirit Island. Unfortunately, the Island is at the far end of the lake, which is only accessible by boat. It is one of the most photographed places in Canada for good reason. Boat tours are available near the parking lot. The best light is usually later in the day. If possible try to catch the last boat trip of the day, as there are fewer ripples in the lake and often the boat crew may allow a little longer stop at the viewing area.

Further east along Route 16 is Miette Hot Springs. Miette Hot Springs is my favorite of the three hot springs in the Canadian Rockies. It is rarely crowded, has amazing mountain views, is quiet, has two big comfortable hot pools, cold plunge pools and one is often greeted by mountain goats in the parking lot. It is located about 40 miles (65km) from Jasper, and well worth the drive.

Maligne Canyon

Medicine Lake

Spirit Island, Maligne Lake

Miette Hot Springs

Maligne Canyon

Emerald Lake

CHAPTER 9 YOHO EMERALD LAKE

Yoho National Park sits to the west of Banff National Park in British Columbia and in the Pacific Time Zone (one hour behind Alberta (which can make a difference if lucky enough to have an appointment to go to Lake Ohara)). Yoho is the smallest of the four National Parks in the Canadian Rockies. Emerald Lake is a 40 minute drive from Lake Louise and makes a nice day trip.

There are many backcountry trails to explore in Yoho. Some of the easier sights to see include: Emerald Lake, Kicking Horse Falls, Takkakaw Falls, the town of Field, and Lake Ohara. With the exception of Lake Ohara, most of these sights can be seen over 1 or two days. Lake Ohara is just plain hard to get to, and it's that way on purpose to limit human impact. The scenery and hiking around Lake Ohara is some of the best in the Canadian Rocks but getting there

can be a real challenge. Reservations for the Lake Ohara Lodge need to be made a full year (or two) in advance. The campground also fills up fast and there are very limited seats on the bus that traverse the private mile access road. If you can get there, the experience is well worth it.

Emerald Lake is just another glacier lake, another over-the-top, amazing glacier lake. This lovely lake is surrounded by mountains of the President Range and by Mount Burgess. The lake has the same surreal blue glow of other glacier fed lakes in the Canadian Rockies. The light here can be amazing. Like Bow Lake, the light at both sunrise and sunset illuminates the surrounding mountains. A trail circles the lake and is wide and flat. At 3.2 mi (5.2 km), it is an easy walk, allowing amazing views of the lodge and mountains. The Emerald Lake

Lodge is a great place to stay and less expensive that it might first appear. Canoes can be rented during the day from the boathouse next to the parking lot. Several restaurants are part of the lodge and serve good food with amazing views.

Mount Burgess is home to the Burgess Shale, which is one of the world's most celebrated fossil sites. The fossils are from the Cambrian Period, approximately 500 million years ago. The fossils are famed for preserving imprints from the softer parts of ancient animals. The area is closed to amateur fossil hunters as serious paleontologists study it.

On the way to Emerald Lake, Emerald Lake Road passes the thundering Kicking Horse Falls. The Kicking Horse river funnels through a narrow channel and shoots out into the basin below. A natural bridge spans the river over this loud channel. I have seen sightseers clamber across this narrow strip of rock. However, a misstep here would be almost certain death, so best to view from further away. This best light here is late in the day, when the surrounding mountains are not backlit.

Takkakaw Falls is another must see in Yoho. This falls originates from the Daly Glacier far above and is hidden from view when at the base of the falls. The name is roughly translated from Cree as "it is magnificent" and it really is. At 991 ft (300 M) it is only the 45th tallest waterfall in British Columbia. Hard to believe that this thundering nearly 1000 foot falls is 45th on the list! After turning onto Yoho Valley Road drive 7 mi (12 km) up a twisty mountain road to the parking area. Paved trails allow easy access to the river and base of the falls. Approaching the base of the falls is magnificent but be prepared to get drenched by spray. Afternoon and evening are the best times to photograph the falls. Often near sunset on clear days, a bright rainbow appears in the mist at the base of the falls. Several backcountry trails take off from the parking area.

The town of Field sits on the highway leading from Banff. This small town has served the passing railway since its beginning. Several hotels and restaurants offer service in Field. Some of the charm of this town is the well-landscaped yards of the 160 residents. This may sound like a strange reason to stop with so much grandeur all around, but a quiet evening stroll through this quaint town provides a peaceful end after a busy day of hiking.

Takakkaw Falls

Emerald Lake

Emerald Lake Lodge

Emerald Lake

Kicking Horse Falls

Takakkaw Falls

Near Field

Field

CHAPTER 10 TRAVEL TIPS

The number one travel tip is: GET THERE SOON! When thinking of the Canadian Rockies, many people think of the famous train tour through the region. While taking the train would be lovely, it would be over too soon and would seem to restrict exploring, and there is so much to explore. So many different areas, lakes, canyons, hikes, hot springs, waterfalls and quiet meadows fill these parks that exploring them by car seems like the best option.

Itineraries of 2-3 days will allow access to some of the best scenery, but will likely leave you hungry for more. If on a short trip, hit the Banff Area, Lake Louise and Bow Lake and take a quick trip into Yoho to see Emerald Lake. If you have a week, spend a day or near Banff Townsite, then 2-3 days near Lake Louise and Bow Lake. If longer time is available,

head north to Jasper and consider a stop at Mt Robson Provincial Park. Having visited this area 8 or 9 times I have never run out of things to see and do, and the variable weather makes some sights more or less accessible with each trip. Even if time is limited try go beyond the views from the care. Take a short hike.

As with higher elevations, the weather is changeable, often changing several times in a day. It can be very hard to predict. We have been snowed on in July (though it didn't accumulate), rained on extensively and once had poor air quality due to a forest fire in the next province, though sunny clear skies directly above. Even if the weather is less than ideal, get out into it. If dressed properly, a little rain won't spoil the day. If you really hate the weather it typically changes quickly and often the changes can be some of

Bow Lake

Apen Leaves

the most beautiful times to view the mountains.

Since these National Parks are pretty big and driving times can add up. When planning a trip it is worthwhile to factor in driving times so the whole trip isn't in the car. When visiting Banff, and arriving in Calgary, I am always tempted to visit Jasper as well. However, if traveling for less than a week this leads to a lot of time in the car. It is hard to overstate how big this region is.

Banff can be enjoyed on a shoestring budget, but also offers chances to relax in the lap of luxury. It also caters to just about every budget in between. Camping is excellent and cheap. Groceries are available in Banff and the Lake Louise Village, but are cheaper in Canmore, cheaper still in Calgary. For luxury, consider a splurge on the Banff Springs Hotel or Chateau Lake Louise. Or, for a quieter, more rustic setting consider

a stay at the luxurious Moraine Lake Lodge.

From paved handicap accessible trails, to short day hikes, or backpacking trails and true mountaineering, there are hiking experiences for everyone.

Parker Ridge Trail

Athabsca Falls Gorge

Iris

Icefields Parkway

Bear Cub

CHAPTER 11 WILDLIFE

Wildlife is everywhere in the Canadian Rockies. It is almost impossible to travel this region and not encounter wild animals. Elk and deer sightings are very common, even within the Town of Banff. The best viewing opportunities are typically early in the morning and near dusk. While driving, keep one eye on the road and the other looking for animals, at least partly for safety reasons.

Always remember that wild animals are wild, often others around seem to forget that. A bear or bull elk can cause serious injury and move much faster than humans. Black bears are more commonly encountered than grizzlies. Usually, the difference is easy to spot due to the color, grizzlies are browner, but sometimes black bears can also be brown. Grizzlies have a distinctive

hump at the base of their neck and tend to be larger. Any bear can be dangerous, but grizzlies tend to be more aggressive and should definitely be avoided. If you see a bear, especially a grizzly, stay in the car. When hiking, travel in groups and make a lot of noise. This helps to avoid startling bears and allows them the opportunity to move away. Bear spray, a concentrated pepper spray, is available, but generally not necessary. Also, please don't feed the animals. At times it is obvious that other have fed them and it puts both the animal and other people at risk.

Another trick is to look for stopped cars at the side of the road to find wildlife, but be careful not to block traffic or get struck by other vehicles passing by. In Banff National Park, I have had the most luck seeing wildlife along

Bighorn Sheep

the Lake Minnewanka Loop, the Bow Valley Parkway and The access road to the Sunshine Village. In Jasper the road to Patricia Lake and Maligne Lake tend to be wildlife hotspots. A campground on the Icefields Parkway is named Wapiti, a Native American word for elk. An elk herd frequents the campground and it is quite an experience waking up surrounded by elk.

Bull Elk in Jasper

Back Bear

Deer

Mountain Goat

Grizzly Bear

Elk Bull

Made in the USA
Lexington, KY
26 June 2019